Content Curation

*To my wife, Melissa; my daughters,
Reaghan and Chesney.*

*And to the countless number of educators who
have helped me learn along the way.*

Content Curation: How to Avoid Information Overload
By Steven W. Anderson @web20classroom

5 Powerful Skills for the Global Learner
By Mark Barnes @markbarnes19

Teaching the iStudent: A Quick Guide to Using Mobile Devices and Social Media
    in the K-12 Classroom
By Mark Barnes @markbarnes19

Connected Leadership: It's Just a Click Away
By Spike Cook @DrSpikeCook

All Hands on Deck: Tools for Connecting Educators, Parents, and Communities
By Brad Currie @bradmcurrie

The Missing Voices in EdTech: Bringing Diversity Into EdTech
By Rafranz Davis @RafranzDavis

Flipping Leadership Doesn't Mean Reinventing the Wheel
By Peter DeWitt @PeterMDeWitt

The Edcamp Model: Powering Up Professional Learning
By the Edcamp Foundation @EdcampUSA

Worlds of Making: Best Practices for Establishing a Makerspace for Your School
By Laura Fleming @NMHS_lms

Leading Professional Learning: Tools to Connect and Empower Teachers
By Tom Murray @thomascmurray and Jeff Zoul @Jeff_Zoul

Empowered Schools, Empowered Students: Creating Connected and Invested Learners
By Pernille Ripp @pernilleripp

Blogging for Educators: Tips for Getting Connected
By Starr Sackstein @mssackstein

Principal Professional Developlment: Leading Learning in the Digital Age
By Joseph Sanfelippo @Joesanfelippofc and Tony Sinanis @TonySinanis

The Power of Branding: Telling Your School's Story
By Tony Sinanis @TonySinanis and Joseph Sanfelippo @Joesanfelippofc

The Relevant Educator: How Connectedness Empowers Learning
By Tom Whitby @tomwhitby and Steven W. Anderson @web20classroom

Content Curation

How to Avoid Information Overload

Steven W. Anderson

CORWIN
A SAGE Company

FOR INFORMATION:

Corwin
A SAGE Company
2455 Teller Road
Thousand Oaks, California 91320
(800) 233-9936
www.corwin.com

SAGE Publications Ltd.
1 Oliver's Yard
55 City Road
London EC1Y 1SP
United Kingdom

SAGE Publications India Pvt. Ltd.
B 1/I 1 Mohan Cooperative Industrial Area
Mathura Road, New Delhi 110 044
India

SAGE Publications Asia-Pacific Pte. Ltd.
3 Church Street
#10-04 Samsung Hub
Singapore 049483

Printed in the United States of America

A catalog record of this book is available from the Library of Congress.

ISBN 978-1-4833-8026-1

This book is printed on acid-free paper.

Executive Editor: Arnis Burvikovs
Associate Editor: Ariel Price
Editorial Assistant: Andrew Olson
Production Editor: Amy Schroller
Copy Editor: Allan Harper
Typesetter: C&M Digitals (P) Ltd.
Proofreader: Laura Webb
Cover and Interior Design: Janet Kiesel
Marketing Manager: Lisa Lysne

SUSTAINABLE FORESTRY INITIATIVE
Certified Chain of Custody
Promoting Sustainable Forestry
www.sfiprogram.org
SFI-01268

SFI label applies to text stock

15 16 17 18 19 10 9 8 7 6 5 4 3 2 1

Contents

Preface

Welcome to the Corwin Connected Educators Series.

Last year, Ariel Price, Arnis Burvikovs, and I assembled a great list of authors for the Fall 2014 books in the Corwin Connected Educators Series. As leaders in their field of connected education, they all provided practical, short books that helped educators around the world find new ways to connect. The books in the Spring 2015 season will be equally as beneficial for educators.

We have all seen momentous changes for educators. States debate the use of the Common Core State Standards, and teachers and leaders still question the use of technology, while some of their students have to disconnect and leave it at home because educators do not know how to control learning on devices. Many of the series authors worked in schools where they were sometimes the only ones trying to encourage use of technology tools at the same time their colleagues tried to ban it. Through their PLNs they were able to find others who were trying to push the envelope.

This spring, we have a list of authors who are known for pushing the envelope. Some are people who wrote books for the Fall 2014 season, while others are brand new to the series. What they have in common is that they see a different type of school for students, and they write about ideas that all schools should be practicing now.

Rafranz Davis discusses *The Missing Voices in EdTech.* She looks at and discusses how we need to bring more diverse voices to the connected world because those voices will enrich how we learn and the way we think. Starr Sackstein, a teacher in New York City writes about blogging for reflection in her book *Blogging for Educators.* Twitter powerhouse Steven W. Anderson returns to the Series to bring us *Content Curation,* as do the very engaging Joseph M. Sanfelippo and Tony Sinanis with their new book, *Principal Professional Development.* Mark Barnes rounds out the comeback authors with his book on *5 Skills for the Global Learner.* Thomas C. Murray and Jeffrey Zoul bring a very practical "how to" for teachers and leaders in their book *Leading Professional Learning,* and Makerspaces extraordinaire Laura Fleming brings her expertise with *Worlds of Making.*

I am insanely excited about this book series. As a former principal I know time is in short supply, and teachers and leaders need something they can read today and put into practice tomorrow. That is the exciting piece about technology; it can help enhance your practices by providing you with new ideas and helping you connect with educators around the world.

The books can be read in any order, and each will provide information on the tools that will keep us current in the digital age. We also look forward to continuing the series with more books from experts on connectedness.

As Michael Fullan has been saying for many years, technology is not the right driver, good pedagogy is, and the books in this connected series focus on practices that will lead to good pedagogy in our digital age. To assist readers in their connected experience, we have created the Corwin Connected Educators companion website where readers can connect with the authors and find resources to help further their experience. The website can be found at www.corwin. com/connectededucators. It is our hope that we can meet you where you are in your digital journey, and bring you up to the next level.

Peter M. DeWitt, EdD @PeterMDeWitt

About the Author

 **Steven W. Anderson** is a learner, speaker, blogger, tweeter, and dad. As a former teacher and Director of Instructional Technology, he is highly sought after for his expertise in educational technology integration and using social media for learning. Represented as @web20classroom, he regularly travels the country talking to schools and districts about the use of social media in the classroom and how to better serve students through technology. Steven has been a presenter and speaker at several educational technology conferences, including ISTE, International Society for Technology in Education; ASCD, Association for Supervision and Curriculum Development; FETC, Florida Educational Technology Conference; VSTE, Virginia Society for Technology in Education; and numerous state and local conferences. He is also responsible for helping to create #edchat, a weekly education discussion on Twitter that boasts over 500 weekly participants. For his work with #edchat, Steven was recognized with the 2009 and 2011 Edublogs, Twitterer of The Year Award along with a 2013 Bammy Award, which is recognized worldwide as the Educational Emmy.

Introduction

sat, staring at my computer screen. Working on a lesson centered around the periodic table, I was struggling to find a video that I had seen in a training session just a week earlier. I poured over my notes, looked back in my Evernote, and even tried searching the Web for some key phrases from the video.

Nothing.

I spent hours like this in my classroom when I was teaching. I would encounter so many great resources from the web, documents from professional development sessions I had attended, notes from meetings—I had information and data scattered all over the place and no real sense to how it should or could be organized.

I saw the same with my students.

I taught middle school students. To me, these are the best students to teach. Watching them transition from elementary to high school was great for me. But their skills at finding good information and storing it for later were haphazard at best. After assigning a project, I'd have to spend more time helping them find and save the best information to suit their needs than they spent doing the actual project. Granted, those skills are important, but they should be emphasized long before middle school.

I encounter this same problem when I talk to educators from across the globe. We have access to a great deal of information for planning lessons, engaging content for our students, and resources to help us be better educators.

We are inundated with vast amounts of information each day. Daniel J. Levitin, in his book entitled *The Organized Mind: Thinking Straight In An Age Of Information Overload,* noted that we took in five times as much information in 2011 as we did in 1986. That is the equivalent of 175 newspapers of data, each and every day![1] And those numbers are sure to get larger with the ever-increasing use of social media and other Internet sources.

If you were to take all of the information attributed to you (your own knowledge, information about you, information related to you, etc.) and wrote it down on 3 × 5 index cards, front and back, you'd have enough cards to cover the entire states of Connecticut and Massachusetts. Try organizing that information in a logical way. Quite the task, if you ask me.

There is a great need for better organization and retrieval of all information, but, for educators and students, there is a specific need for better management of digital assets. During my time using social media, I have discovered that finding information is not a problem. Again, I am inundated with resources whenever I sign in. Using Twitter or reading blogs, it is easy to find the information and data that I am looking for. What is needed is a great system for organizing all of these resources and then, more importantly, an easy way to share this information with others.

Think about the job of a museum curator. The curator's task is to find and build exhibits that tell some sort of story. The curator scours the research to find the best information and then presents it to the public in a logical way. To boil it down to three parts, the curator's job is to collect, organize, and share information.

The same is true of educators and students. We are all researching, reading, and collecting massive amounts of data that we ultimately will want to use for some purpose. As educators, for example, we might want to save a particular video to use in a lesson on the periodic table. Similarly, students need to learn the most effective ways to organize and retrieve their research so they can create new knowledge.

Take Problem-Based Learning for example. Both the teacher and the student have a need to better organize and share information. The teacher needs to find sites, examples, helpful resources, and so on., that will assist students as they navigate through their problem. Students will gather many resources on their own that they will need to recall later or will apply different resources to different solutions. Both the teacher and the students also need an easy way to share these resources with each other because the information does no good if it is simply hoarded.

In this book, we will explore what curation is and how it is done. We'll examine the role that curation plays in professional growth and learning for educators and how curation can be done in the classroom. Most importantly, we will look several digital tools in depth to help make curation and sharing easier.

Note

1. Levitin, D. J. Chapter 1. *The organized mind: Thinking straight in the age of information overload.* New York: Dutton Adult, 2014. p. 6.

What Is Curation?

In its simplest form, curation involves three parts. The first part is the actual finding of the information that we are after. The next part is the storage of that information in a logical way. The last, and most important, part is to share what we find. As easy as it sounds, there are many considerations and skills that educators and students need—specifically, information literacy skills that will help to find the best information, check it for validity, and share it in the best way.

Let's look at each of the three parts of curation in more detail.

THE RIGHT INFORMATION AT THE RIGHT TIME

Finding information might seem easy. Hop onto the Internet, go to your favorite search engine, and a search box with a blinking cursor will be waiting for you to put it to work. You type in your search, and millions upon millions of results are returned. Look at a simple search for "World War 2." At the time of writing this sentence, there were over 341,000,000 returned results on Google. And if you were to do the same search after reading this sentence, odds are that the number will have increased as new information is being found every day and our knowledge of subjects and topics continues to get deeper and wider.

Finding the information you need quickly and efficiently is important now more than ever. When it comes to searching the Web or specific websites, there are few helpful tricks that you can employ yourself and also teach to your students.

- **Simplify Your Search.** Entering long strings of words or questions into search boxes not only makes your work harder, it doesn't return better results. Sometimes less is more. Ask yourself if there is a way that you can simplify what you are looking for into just a few words or a phrase.

- **Search-Friendly Words.** Many search engines suggest using words that appear on webpages rather than the common spoken-language words that we use in conversation. For example, Google suggests using "headache" instead of "my head hurts" because the medical sites that have the information you are probably looking for will use the medical term rather than the conversational term.

- **Get Familiar With Advanced Search.** Most search engines have advanced options. Take time to learn what those advanced options are, because they can be powerful. Google allows you to get very specific with your advanced search by looking at just a specific set of websites, excluding other sites, narrowing the search results by the type of resource (PDF, PPT, DOC, etc.), and much more. These advanced search options can help you to find what you are looking for much more quickly and efficiently than a generic search can.

Social media has only added to our depth of understanding. Services like Twitter allow us to see news as it is breaking in real time or to follow historical events as if they were happening in real time. Take the sinking of the Titanic. The Twitter account @TitanicRealTime (https://twitter.com/TitanicRealTime) tweets the events related to the Titanic—from the historic building of the ship, to the launch and sinking, to the rescue efforts—each year on the days and times when these events actually happened. Even students are getting into the act by creating accounts for historical figures, examining how they would have used social media if these tools had been around when they were alive.

You don't have to live on social media in order find what you are looking for. Just like using a search engine like Google or Bing to find information, many social media sites have search capabilities as well. Of these, Twitter Search (http://search.twitter.com) is the most feature-rich. Not only can you search the timelines of specific users or hashtags, you can simply enter what you are looking for and use the advanced search options to look for tweets that contain your information from a specific place or that have a happier or sadder tone.

It bears repeating that, in the classroom, students need many opportunities to practice looking for the best information for a subject and using these skills to find it. Later on, we will look at a few lessons plans that you can use in the classroom to help students at all levels perform better searches.

LET'S GET ORGANIZED

The next part of the curation process after finding the information is figuring out what to do with it. Later on, we will look at some very handy tools that you can use to organize what you find. But first, how do you decide, once you find something, if it's worth saving? We must use our information literacy skills not only to find the best information but also to determine if that information suits our needs and if the information is reliable.

I get asked all the time how I determine, when I find a resource, that I want to save it. Usually, I find it very difficult to answer that question. In the past, I saved 99% of the resources that I found. I figured that I would have a use for it at some point, so I might as well save it. Recently, I've discovered that doing so only causes me confusion and information overload. If you save everything you find, you're not utilizing your information literacy skills to weed out the stuff you don't really need while also cluttering up what you are curating with junk, which makes it harder to find the best stuff you have saved.

What are the information literacy skills you need to ensure you are saving only the best information?

- **What's Your Goal?** Ask yourself, why do I need this resource? Is it for something I am working on? Do I need it for an upcoming lesson or would it complement a lesson I've already taught that I can use next time? Have a point to your search and stay focused.

- **When Will You Use It?** Because Twitter and other social search engines allow you to find information on a wide variety of topics, it's easy for you to get overloaded with really great information. When you find the perfect blog post or video or website, ask yourself, "If I save this, when will I use it?" Because information changes so rapidly and new information comes along, it is easy for something that seemed so good at first to go stale very fast. Therefore, consider when you will use the resource and how fresh it's going to be when you use it.

- **Just How Good Is It?** One of the most important aspects of information literacy when you are examining a resource to determine whether or not you should keep it is to determine its validity. Again, the rapid pace at which information changes and new data are discovered has made some information unreliable. Look at your resource. Can you confirm it comes from a source you trust? Can the information contained in the resource be validated with another source? Primary sources are usually the best, but secondary sources can be just as good. Just be sure to do your homework and make sure that the resource is all that it says it is.

Howard Rheingold is an author and educator who has been speaking about information literacy since the early days of the Internet. In his many books, he discusses the need for the general public to have a filter when it comes to all of the information that we encounter daily. Rheingold calls it "crap detection." As Rheingold states,

> Unless a great many people learn the basics of online crap detection and begin applying their critical faculties en masse and very soon, I fear for the future of the Internet as a useful source of credible news, medical advice, financial information, educational resources, scholarly and scientific research. Some critics argue that a tsunami of hogwash has already rendered the Web useless. I disagree. We are indeed inundated by online noise pollution, but the problem is soluble. The good stuff is out there if you know how to find and verify it. Basic information literacy, widely distributed, is the best protection for the knowledge commons: A sufficient portion of critical consumers among the online population can become a strong defense against the noise-death of the Internet. (http://blog.sfgate.com/rheingold/2009/06/30/crap-detection-101/)

Rheingold goes on to describe how crap detection became important as his teenage daughter was beginning to use the Internet to find information. At that time, we could generally trust the information published in books because the information was edited and verified by publishers and professionals. The digital age and the Internet changed all that. Then and now, anyone can get a free website or blog and say whatever they want. We have to use the best available filter when trying to find the best information.

While this second step in curation is mostly about storing information, understanding how to make sure you are storing the best stuff is important. You wouldn't store trash in your storage locker as it only takes up space and doesn't let you store all the good things you need to save. So when you are curating information, take the time to take out the trash and make room for the best stuff.

SHARE. AND SHARE SOME MORE

When I moved from the classroom to a district-level technology position, I was working in a small district in terms of number of schools (11) but a very large district in terms of geography. From my office, it could take me upwards of 90 minutes to get to the elementary school that was furthest away.

Social media was in its infancy then. I had been reading about microblogging sites such as Twitter in my professional magazines and even had given it a try before abandoning it as just a passing fad. (Boy, was I wrong!) I maintained a blog so that I could share instructional technology strategies or ideas for integrating technology into the classroom with all of my schools without having to travel so far and so often. But even though some individuals were reading the blog, it was tough for many to keep up. That's when I decided to give Twitter another go. I posted items to my own blog as well as other resources that I was finding, and my teachers could either consume that information as I was posting it or revisit it later.

What I found, however, was that the teachers in my district were not the only ones who benefited. Teachers and educators in other schools and districts were reading my tweets, sharing my resources, and benefiting from what I was posting.

I had always been a believer that educators have a moral obligation to share. From the time I stepped foot in a classroom, if I had a good idea (or even the occasional bad one), I wanted to share it so that others could try it and we could learn together. I also believed that all of our students could benefit from this sharing among educators. But there were always a handful of teachers who were hoarders of knowledge. They wanted only their students to benefit, and they wanted all the glory and attention. I didn't have that mindset. While I was teaching my students, if I had an idea that could improve teaching and learning for other students, why wouldn't I share it? Why would I hoard it?

The third step in our curation process is often the one that is most overlooked, but it is equally important as the other steps. If we are spending a great deal of time searching for the best information, finding it, and ensuring its quality, only to keep it under wraps, what good can come of that? Think of the museum curator. If she spent all her time going to the ends of the earth to find the best pieces to tell a story and then didn't share that story with anyone, what was her point in the beginning?

As you will see, sharing plays a prominent role in all of the tools and resources that we are going to examine in depth. We live in an age in which we can not only consume the information we find, we can add to it, manipulate it, catalog it, and then share it with the world so that others can learn from our learning.

Sharing what you curate can be as simple as having a sharing time during your monthly faculty or professional learning community (PLC) meeting. In my time working with educators from across the globe, simply taking five minutes to go around the table and share some great resources can do wonders in helping everyone be better educators as well as in building group and staff morale. Everyone feels like a contributor and feels like he or she has something to offer.

Digital spaces have allowed us to extend our faculty or PLC meeting beyond our own school or district. Facebook, online communities, or professional organization's interest groups connect us to a cadre of other educators who are eager to share and learn together.

Here are a few of my favorite ways to share resources and information I curate:

- **Blogs.** I have a blog (http://blog.web20classroom.org) where I share a lot of my information. I enjoy sharing and reflecting on what I have gathered because it allows others to do the same right along with me. Another new space for me is my Postach.io blog (http://postachio.web20classroom.org) You'll learn more about Postachio later, but it is a really simple and quick way to share what I am finding as well.

- **Twitter.** As you can tell, I do use Twitter (http://twitter.com/web20classroom) for the majority of finding resources, mostly because it's the easiest and quickest way for me. Hashtags have the true power, and many educators learn very quickly when starting out that a great deal of good information is exchanged through hashtags. (Learn more about hashtags: http://blog.web20classroom.org/2011/11/its-all-about-hashtag.html)

- **Online Communities.** As I mentioned, online communities can be a great way not only to find information but also to connect with other educators and curators as well. One of the best places is Edweb.net (http://home.edweb.net). This site boasts several popular communities, including ones for leadership, technology in learning, and others. In addition, it provides me with an excellent platform to share what I am finding and also to learn from others who are sharing their own knowledge.

REFLECTION ACTIVITY

Review the three steps in the curation process (Locate, Organize, Share). Ask yourself the following questions:

1. What are you currently doing well?
2. What do you need improvement in?
3. Look at the resources that you have saved in your bookmarks/favorites in your browser. If they disappeared tomorrow, could you remember all of them? Are they effectively organized?
4. Think about sharing. Do you have a way to share the resources that you are collecting? How are other educators around you sharing their resources?

Curation for
Professional Learning

A s we've discovered, curation is not just finding the resources but organizing them and sharing your learning with the world. As educators, we often perform the task of curation, but many times we give it very little thought. You might be just like me, sitting and staring at your screen, wondering where to begin looking for lesson plan ideas or resources for teaching. And, as we already discovered, there are a number of places to begin and methods to employ.

Curating information or knowledge for use in teaching is, in many ways, similar to curating information or knowledge for your own professional learning. The skill sets and tools that you will use to curate information for lessons are quite similar to those that you will use to curate information for your own professional learning.

In the last chapter, we looked at how blogs, hashtags, and online communities can be great ways to share what you curate. But did you know that these tools can be even more beneficial by helping you to discover content for your own professional learning? Let's examine how each tool can contribute in its own unique way.

BLOGS FOR LEARNING

I have been using blogs to curate knowledge and information for my own professional learning since I have been in education. I was always impressed with what others were willing to share of their own learning journeys that I spent a great deal of time reading blogs. We have learned that blogs are an excellent way to share our own learning, but they can do so much more when we use them to learn from the information shared by others.

The challenge comes when we need to find blogs to read. I had a hard time with that when I was starting out. I would stumble upon a really great blog, but a single blog provided only one perspective. The curator in me wanted to read more blogs, but I had a difficult time finding them. Over the years, I have developed a few tricks to help others get started with finding good blogs to read.

- **Blogrolls.** The great thing about bloggers is that they are often readers of others blogs, which they share freely. When you find a great blog, look to see if it includes a blogroll or a list of other blogs to read. Blogrolls can be a good place to start when you want to build your own set of blogs to read, and part of the curation process has been done for you. The author is sharing these blogs because he or she reads them and finds value in them, and odds are that you will too.
- **Edublog Awards** (http://edublogawards.com/). Each year, the educational blogging service, Edublogs, hosts blog awards. Bloggers nominate the best educational, leadership, and classroom blogs, and the community votes for the winners. These awards can be a gold mine of new content each

year. Much of the first part of the curation process has been done for you. Authors have to provide reasons why they are nominating, so you can see what those reasons are and find the best content for your professional learning.

- **The Teach100 List.** (http://teach.com/teach100) From the University of Southern California, the Teach100 list is a ranking of the best educational blogs. This is another great place to find good blogs to read. I don't believe the rankings mean all that much, but the blogs listed there are the most talked about and shared, so you can be pretty sure that they can provide a great deal of learning for you.

TWITTER HASHTAGS AND CHATS

In the last chapter, we briefly discussed how hashtags can be used to share information that you are curating. When I lead professional development sessions for educators about Twitter or social media in general, I usually begin with the power of hashtags. Hashtags are a simple way to share information with and gather from a specific target group of people.

Hashtags are words or phrases preceded by a hash symbol (#). They were first used in the early days of Twitter as a way for conference-goers to exchange information in a more organized way. Today, hashtags have invaded almost all facets of our lives. You might have seen the hashtag #SuperBowl, which allows views to share thoughts and reactions during the big game. Many television shows, sporting events, and news events have hashtags that provide anyone with the ability to see what others are saying and sharing.

The same is true for educators. Hashtags have become a large part of how educators share and gather information on Twitter. Many hashtags are targeted at specific areas of curriculum (#STEM, #CommonCore, etc.), while others are more general topics in education (#PBL, #BYOD, etc.). Professional organizations and conferences usually have hashtags that you can follow as well. So, while even though you might not be able to attend a large conference, you can still see what people are sharing and saying and learn from that.

Using Twitter Search, you can see the tweets that include specific hashtags, and you don't have to be a registered Twitter user to do so. You can simply visit the search page, type in a hashtag, and begin to see all the rich information that is being shared. You can also see who is tweeting that information, so that, if you do have an account, you can follow that person and never miss a tweet from him or her.

Some hashtags include the word "chat" (#edchat, #4thchat, #scichat). These hashtags normally indicate that there is a regularly scheduled time during which anyone can join in and have a real-time conversation around a specific topic. Twitter chats are another great way to find information and people from whom you can learn and thereby help yourself to grow as a professional. (You will find more detailed resources on hashtags and Twitter chats in the Resources chapter.)

ONLINE COMMUNITIES

My first experience with online communities was a private group in the first district in which I worked. As science teachers, we had a virtual message board where we could post questions and share information. As there were over 150 middle school science teachers spread across many schools, the virtual platform allowed us to learn together without actually having to be face-to-face. I was able to learn a great deal from the experience in our group, and I do believe that it helped me to be a better science teacher as I was starting out.

Today, there are online communities for virtually any topic and subject you can think of that can help you to curate knowledge to add to your own professional learning. What draws many educators to online communities is that they aren't restricted to real time; that is, the educators can check in at any time. There is no sense that they have to be online all the time to benefit. And that is true. You can check in when you have time and find valuable information to enhance your own learning.

While there are many online communities to investigate, a few rise to the surface as some of the best.

- **Classroom 2.0** (http://classroom20.com). This is one of the oldest and largest educator online communities out there. With over 80,000 members, its depth is vast. When you sign up for a free account, you'll get access to forums where you can post questions and share information, specific interest groups that will allow you to go deeper with a subject, and videos on a variety of topics. The site also host webinars and other events that will extend your learning beyond just the community.

- **Edmodo Communities.** Many schools and districts are using Edmodo, a free, private social networking service, to connect students to virtual classrooms. But there is a large community of subject and topic-area groups that you can join as an educator. The groups have many thousands of members who share resources and provide support each and every day. If you are using Edmodo in your school or district (and even if you aren't), the communities can be another great place to learn.

- **EdWeb** (http://home.edweb.net). We already discussed the communities in Edweb, which are great, but the site is really known for its free webinars. Almost every day, you can take part in free webinars focusing on a wide variety of topics— everything from formative assessment to integrating STEM into classroom design. And if you can't join live, you can catch the recordings. This is a place I often go when I am looking for specific learning or when I need to curate information for a specific topic.

REFLECTION ACTIVITIES

1. Review the section on blogging. Visit the Teach100 blog list and find five blogs to read. Set aside 30 minutes, three times a week, to visit those blogs and read the new posts. Open Google Doc, Word, or other word processing program of your choice and write a brief reflection of what you found. You can also use this document to record and organize the resources that you found in those posts.

2. Visit the Edweb.net Communities. Take time to register and to browse the list of communities found there. Join one that provides some value to you because it is relevant either to a topic that you teach or to a topic that you are interested in learning more about. Pay special attention to the webinar calendar, make note of an upcoming webinar, and register to attend. Also, browse the webinar archives for the community. Watch an archived webinar. Go back to the document that you started in Reflection Activity 1. Write a brief reflection, and record and organize the resources found from the webinar.

Tools for Curation

Evernote

When I started teaching, my first classroom was one that had been used by a teacher who had retired the year before. I came in over the summer to move some stuff in and get familiar with my new space. While I was getting settled, I found it. The closet was filled to the brim with folders, books, posters—you name the resource, and it was probably in that closet. To a new teacher, it was like finding the pot of gold at the end of the rainbow. I thought I had won the lottery. All the things that a teacher had collected in over 30 years of teaching was in this closet.

As I came back to reality and really started looking at all this stuff, I realized very quickly that while the closet probably included some treasures, it was going to take me quite a while to go through everything, figure out what was worth saving, and organize it in a useful way.

Fast-forward to the digital age, and many of us are faced with the same daunting task. We are curating so much information from so many different sources, we have our own pot of gold. But trying to organize websites, article clippings, sound recordings, and/or documents can cause some to panic. It can be like looking at that closet full of stuff and not knowing where to start.

It doesn't have to be that way.

I'll admit it. I used to be one of the most unorganized people on the planet. I had notebooks in just about every bag I carried. I had both analog and digital calendars and still missed appointments. I had slips of paper and sticky notes that were covered with strings of illegible thoughts—needless to say, whenever I found these reminders, I did not have a clue what I had been thinking when I wrote them. Not to mention all the digital stuff. Clips of blog posts that I wanted to reference. That perfect image for my next presentation. I had stuff all over the place in a variety of formats that I needed to tame.

I have more than 10 different types of projects going on at any one time. Books, book chapters, keynotes, presentations, consulting projects, product reviews, and on and on and on. Not to mention projects around my home and activities with my daughters.

Organization isn't really in my vocabulary.

Well, perhaps I should say, it *wasn't* in my vocabulary.

But it is now, thanks to Evernote.

> **URL:** http://evernote.com
>
> **Cost:** Free (Premium upgrade available.)

I had tried Evernote a few times in the past. I would install it and look at it and could not really find a use for it. I would uninstall it and go on my way, unorganized, missing appointments, stressing about putting things together. But that is all in the past. I use Evernote every day in so many different ways. I can't live without it. I rely on it so much, it's on every phone, tablet, computer and browser that I use.

HOW DOES IT WORK?

Think back to that closet I encountered in my first classroom. Evernote is a digital closet. This closet includes filing cabinets, and those cabinets are further organized by drawer and folders.

In Evernote, there are three main terms to know:

- **Notebooks.** These are the filing cabinets and/or the drawers within the filing cabinets. Everything you do resides in a notebook, and you can have notebooks within notebooks if you want to get highly and deeply organized.
- **Notes.** These are where your creating or saving happens. Notes are text-like documents that you can write on, attach things to, or embed documents within. You can have as many notes within a notebook as you need.
- **Tags.** Tags are a quick and easy way to filter your notes and find information quickly and efficiently. While you might have your Evernote organized by notes and notebooks, using tags adds another powerful way to organize your stuff.

MY CURRENT LIST OF NOTEBOOKS

I have professional notebooks, personal notebooks, and notebooks for other work that I do. Within those notebooks, I have several other nested notebooks to further organize my stuff. I use the built-in tools like note reminders and checkboxes to make sure that I keep myself on track.

So, you are saying to yourself, "Yeah, Steven, this is great. But what does it have to do with curation?"

It is what you can put in these notes and notebooks that holds the power for curators. Virtually anything can go in a note or notebook.

FIGURE 4.1   Screenshot of My Evernote Notebooks

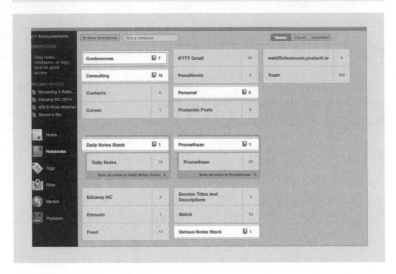

SOURCE: Evernote.com

As we saw, notes are just basic text documents that you can add content to. But what kinds of content? Text, obviously. But images, links, and documents can all be embedded on the page or attached to the note or notebook, just like you would attach something to an email. And, speaking of email, your Evernote account comes with its own email address. You can add content from your email system by simply forwarding the message to your Evernote email address. A note will be created in your default notebook. This feature can be extremely helpful when someone sends you something that you need to save. You can keep your inbox empty, and the note is filed away ready for you to use it when you need it.

But it gets better. One of the features I use a lot is adding audio to notes. I can create a note, add all my content to it, and record a voice note over the top. This is very helpful when I want to remember what I was doing with the note or add in any thoughts that might be helpful.

Notes can be shared directly to many of your social networks right from within Evernote. You can also make your notes public and share the link in a variety of ways. Notebooks can also be shared, and you can invite others to collaborate with on your notes and notebooks.

I keep Evernote open on my computer at all times. I never know when I am going to need it or when it could come in handy. And I have it no matter where I am because Evernote is completely mobile. If you are out and about, you can scan documents or add images straight to your notes from your phone or tablet.

OTHER EVERNOTE SERVICES

Evernote is more than just a program for your laptop or an app on your phone. One of the best features is the Web Clipper. The Evernote Web Clipper extension saves portions of websites or just some text from a blog post that you want to use somewhere else.

The Evernote Web Clipper

As you can see, you have several options with the Web Clipper:

- **Article.** Clips the entire page (including text, images, and videos) and saves it to a notebook that you choose.
- **Simplified Article.** Strips out all of the side bars, ads, and other stuff and leaves just the article.
- **Full Page.** Saves the entire webpage, extra stuff and all.
- **Bookmark.** Saves just a link to the page.
- **Screenshot.** Takes an image of just the selected portion of the page.

You can also directly add tags to your clip and add notes through the Add Remark button. When you use the Web Clipper, your cursor changes into a highlighter, allowing you to mark up the page with highlights before clipping. After clipping, those highlights are saved in the note.

FIGURE 4.2   Screenshot of Evernote Web Clipper

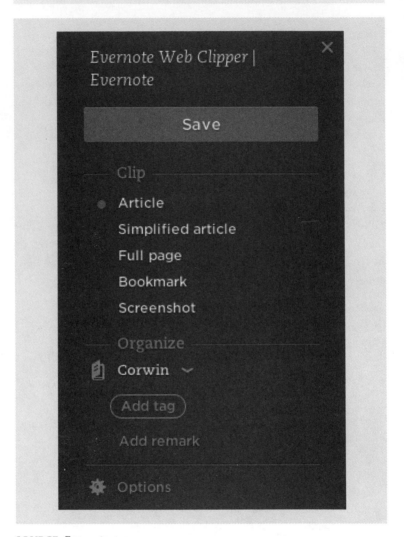

SOURCE: Evernote.com

I use my Web Clipper every day. As I am reading a blog, I can clip quotes or sections that I want to make sure I have. Or I can save images that I may want to use in the future. When you clip something, the link back to the original page is saved too, allowing you to provide a correct citation when you do use the information.

Postach.io

New to the Evernote scene is a third-party service called Postach.io (http://postach.io). I learned about Postach.io through a friend who was raving about how easy it was to take information that had been gathered in Evernote and post it to the web. I gave it a look, and now I am hooked!

Postach.io is a publishing platform that uses a notebook in your Evernote account as the source of your posts. Posts come in the form of notes that you create. When you add a "published" tag, the posts are automatically fed to your free Postach.io site, formatted nicely, and shared with the world.

Postach.io really offers a simple way to take articles that you've clipped, organize them into a note, add some additional thoughts, and publish them for the world to reflect on. For some, setting up a blog to share information that they curate can seem like a complex task. With Postach.io, all of the work is done in Evernote—Postach.io does all the work for you!

You can see from my Postach.io blog (http://postachio.web20class room.org) that I have short posts of things that I am finding and want to share. Since Evernote is where a lot of these things end up as I find them, it only makes sense that when I wanted to share them I set up a Postach.io site. Within a matter of moments, I took lots of information that was locked away in my Evernote notebooks and was able to share it with the world.

EVERNOTE IN THE CLASSROOM

As you can see, Evernote can be a powerful tool for helping you to organize what you are curating as an educator. But Evernote can do the same for students. One idea is to use Evernote as a Cloud-based portfolio where students can store their resources. Because of Evernote's ability to accept lots of different kinds of inputs (text, images, audio, files, PDFs, etc.), it is a perfect addition to the portfolio-based classroom. The same is true for teachers. If you are an administrator, think about it. Since notebooks can be shared, you could create a notebook for each teacher, share the notebook with the teacher, and use the notebook as a place to gather evaluation materials throughout the year. Simple and elegant. (Visit the Resources section to see how you can use Evernote in the classroom to help students organize their curated information.)

REFLECTION ACTIVITY

1. Sign up for a free Evernote Account and add the Web Clipper to your browser. As you are reading the blogs from the Chapter 3 Reflection Activity, practice clipping your favorite passages and pieces from the articles.
2. In your Evernote account, create a notebook for the reflections you've been entering into a Google Doc or Word document. Either attach these reflections or copy and paste them to a note. Continue those reflection activities using the Notes feature in your Reflection Activity notebook.

Tools for Curation

Diigo

My first classroom was in a technology-rich environment. Each teacher had a laptop that he or she could use to do work both at home and at school. I also had a computer to use in my classroom for teaching, and all of these computers were connected by a high-speed, fairly advanced computer network. If I logged onto one computer and saved some information, I could access the information from another computer, provided I was on the same network.

The same was true for favorites or bookmarks in my web browser. If I was researching lesson plan ideas for my class, I could bookmark those sites in my browser and, no matter which computer I logged onto in the district, I had access to those sites. It was very handy, provided I was at a school. When I went home, I didn't have access to those resources, which proved challenging.

Online bookmarking or, as it is more widely known, social book-marking, has been around since 1996. In the early days of the World Wide Web, scientists had public electronic bulletin boards to which they could post links. Social bookmarking really took off in 2003 with the launch of a site called Del.icio.us (Delicious) and other similar sites. Fast-forward to today, and many options are available.

Social bookmarking allows users to do three very important tasks. The first is to save bookmarks and favorites using a variety of methods and access those saves from any device that is connected to the Internet (also known as the Cloud). Now, if I was saving a website at school using one of these services, it wouldn't matter whether I was connected to the school network. Since these sites reside in the Cloud, it doesn't matter where I am—as long as I am connected to the Internet, I can get to my information.

The second important task that social bookmarking allows is the tagging of resources. Tagging is one of the most important parts of the curation process. Think about all of the information that we gather in a day. Try remembering specific parts of that information, such as the title, summary, or exact URL of a particular resource. I might remember some of this information, but remembering all of it would be impossible. Tagging does that work for you. If I had saved my periodic table video and tagged it as "periodic table" in my social bookmarking site, I wouldn't need to remember the title or anything else about the video. I would simply remember the tag.

Last, social bookmarking services are called "social" for a reason. These sites allow you to easily share your information with others. While you can choose to keep some or all of your collection private, as educators, shouldn't we be sharing our knowledge and resources with others? Social bookmarking sites allow you to do that very easily, either through the site itself or through social media services like Twitter, Facebook, and others.

As mentioned, when it comes to social bookmarking services, you have lots of options available. For educators, there is one option that works incredibly well for a variety of reasons, and that's Diigo.

- **URL:** http://diigo.com
- **Steven's Public Diigo:** http://diigo.com/user/stevenanderson
- **Cost:** Free (Free upgrade for educators. Paid/Premium Options available)

Diigo has been around since 2006 and is a very popular choice for educators because of the many free options that it offers. Diigo is, at its core, a social bookmarking service. Diigo allows the user to easily accomplish the three core tasks that I described earlier (saving, tagging, and sharing).

HOW DOES IT WORK?

A user begins by navigating to a webpage that he or she wants to save. Then, using the Diigo bookmarklet or Diigo browser extension, the user can save that page to his or her Diigo Library. (See the Resources section for a video tutorial.)

FIGURE 5.1   Screenshot of the Diigo Chrome Web Browser Extension

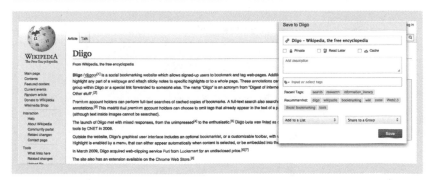

SOURCE: Diigo.com

When you choose to save a webpage to your Diigo library, you have several options. You give the page a name (the name is usually pulled in automatically, but you have the option to change it), add a description if you like, and, most importantly, add tags. The browser extension and bookmarklet will auto-suggest tags for you to use, or your can type in others.

Another, important option is to make the save private. Remember that the saves in your Diigo account are public unless you mark them as private. There may be times when you want to keep some resources private, such as resources that are more personal or those that you just don't want others to see. Whatever the reason, you have the option here to make it private.

The Diigo Browser extension has lots of other great features too.

FIGURE 5.2 Screenshot Showing All of the Options in the Diigo Chrome Web Browser Extension

SOURCE: Diigo.com

In addition to saving a page to your library, you have options such as "Read Later," which allows you to privately save a page to a read-later list. The item is saved to your master library, but you will be able to get back to it later using the "Unread" filter in your library and have the option to save it to your library after you have checked it out.

A very handy feature in this menu is "Annotate." This allows you to mark up a page with a virtual highlighter and save just that portion of the page. This feature is great when you want to save a snippet from an article. You also can add virtual sticky notes to pages, which can be used as notes. So, when someone clicks a link from your public library, he or she can see your annotations (i.e., your highlights or sticky notes), provided that you've made them public. This is a great feature for administrators who want to share specific sections of articles with faculty or for teachers who want to share notes on resources for students.

As you can see, Diigo has a many, many useful features. For example, the "Screenshot" feature allows you to take screenshots of pages, draw and write on them, and save them to your library, and the "Share This Page" feature allows you to share the page with your social networks right from the extension or search all of Diigo without ever leaving the current page.

The "My Library" feature is the hub of your Diigo account. The library includes all of the pages, annotations, and sites that you had marked for later reading. Items are organized according to the order in which they were added (with the last added item appearing first), but there are powerful sorting options that allow you to see just annotations, screenshots, read or unread items, and so on. You can also browse your most popular tags to see resources that way.

Most important, from the "My Library" tab, you have the ability to search your saved bookmarks. Remember the tags that we added to our save previously? I can type the name of a tag, and it instantly appears. Don't remember the tag but remember a part of the URL? Not a problem! Using the Advanced Search function, I can search using multiple tags, parts of the URL, or even words or phrases found in the body of the webpage. Powerful stuff!

FIGURE 5.3 Screenshot of the "My Library" Tab

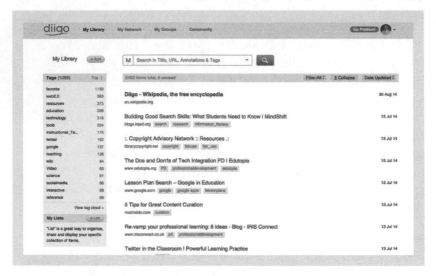

SOURCE: Diigo.com

Because Diigo is social, you can follow other Diigo users and get updates when they add new items to their libraries. Under your "My Network" tab, you can see all of the users you are following, along with any recent additions to their public libraries. You can also find new Diigo users to follow or connect your social media accounts to see if any of your colleagues are also using the service. Seeing what others are sharing is a great way for me to find new content or to find content to share with others.

By far, one of my favorite features of Diigo is the "My Groups" feature, which allows users with similar interests to share resources. You can get daily or weekly emails of resources added to your group and use your group to build your professional learning network. From the "My Groups" tab, you can see all the groups you belong to, see suggested groups, and browse for new ones.

FIGURE 5.4 Screenshot of the "My Network" Tab

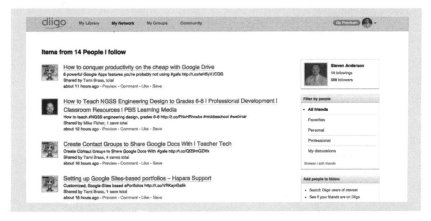

SOURCE: Diigo.com

FIGURE 5.5 Screenshot of the "My Groups" Tab

SOURCE: Diigo.com

USING DIIGO IN THE CLASSROOM

Diigo is a great tool to use in the classroom because of the additional features it offers to educators. When you visit the Diigo Educator Accounts page (http://diigo.com/education) you can receive a free upgrade to your account by answering a few questions. Once approved, you will have several new options that will allow you to better use Diigo in your classroom.

- **Student Accounts.** Upgraded educator accounts have the ability to create student accounts with just a few easy steps. Simply type in students' names or import them via a file that you create, and your students will instantly have a Diigo account. Students do not need email addresses in order to have an account. However, if they do, you can invite them via email as well.

- **Class Groups.** When you import students' accounts, they are all automatically added to the same, private group, which allows the students to share their curated resources with each other. You can further break them down into smaller groups for projects or other activities.

REFLECTION ACTIVITY

1. Sign up for a free Diigo account. (Upgrade to an Educator account if you are eligible.) Take the resources that you gathered in the Chapter 3 and 4 Reflection Activities and save them to your Diigo account.

2. Visit the Communities section of Diigo. Browse the Communities and find one of interest to you. Sign up to receive weekly emails of all the resources added there.

Tools for Curation

Pocket

Back when I started out using Twitter and reading blogs for my professional growth, there were not too many people doing the same. Sure, there was lots of great information to find, but the rate at which it was coming to me was something I could easily manage. As more and more educators discovered the power that these resources had on their learning, I was faced with a flood of great information that I had to manage.

For a while, I was using Twitter Favorites. But that became a challenge. Twitter Favorites are public because my account is public. However, there were some sites that I wanted to vet before I added them to a public list and there were some resources I simply wanted to keep private. And if the tweet that included what I wanted to save was deleted, my Favorite was deleted too. I needed a way to keep what I was finding private for a short time so that I could evaluate the resource before adding it to a public list and a way to ensure that I could find the resource when I needed it.

Sounds like Diigo, right? I can save a link to my library, make it private, evaluate it, and then make it public. At the time, that was complex process, and the process wasn't integrated into Twitter. So, Diigo wasn't the right tool for me.

I stumbled across a simple app called Pocket (at the time it was called ReadItLater, but it has since changed names). Pocket is similar to Diigo as it allows you to save sites to a list, but in Pocket, that list is automatically private. Pocket is integrated into many applications, so I just need to sign into my account and start saving, which makes it great for when I want to save links from Twitter or read blogs through an app on my tablet.

As we looked at earlier, part of the curation process is to examine what we save in order to ensure that it meets a that need we have. If it doesn't, then we remove it to make room for other resources. Because of the rate at which I can get information from sources such as Twitter, blogs, and other social media sites, I often don't have time to vet those resources as they come in. Using Pocket gives me the option to still save the link but to evaluate it before sharing it with others.

- **URL:** http://getpocket.com
- **Cost:** Free (Premium/Paid option available)

HOW DOES IT WORK?

To begin, you create a free account. You then install the free browser extension or bookmarklet to your favorite web browser. Once installed, the process of saving a page is simple. Click the icon in your browser, and your page is saved so you can read it later. You have the option to tag your save so that you can search for it later.

When you sign in, you get an almost magazine-like view of the items you've saved. Once in your library, you have several sorting options, like searching by the tags you've added, or, more generically, like browsing through the webpages, videos, or images you've saved. You have a great deal of control over the way items are presenting to you for review.

When you click on something that you want to read or view, the article or item is stripped down to just the bare elements. No sidebars or ads, just the title, text, and any images embedded in the piece. All of the distractions from the original page are gone, allowing you to focus on just the important information. You can also change the type of text, the size of the text, and the background color, depending on your needs. And you always have the option to view the original site if you need to.

Once done with an article, you can choose to mark it as read, add tags, add it to a favorites list, or delete it altogether. There are also built-in sharing options, allowing you to post articles to your connected social networks or email articles to your address book.

One of my favorite features is the "Read" list. While the "Unread" list is where saved items go, once you mark an item as read it gets moved to the Read list. This list becomes a rich repository of items that I've forgotten about or that I didn't remember to add to my Diigo account to save permanently. Having this Read list has saved me a time or two when I remembered that I had saved something but couldn't find it anywhere. The same search controls that you have in your Unread list are available in your Read list, so finding items is just as easy.

While I primarily use Pocket on my laptop or desktop, it is mobile-friendly as well. There are apps for all types of mobile devices. Your account syncs up to your apps so you can read your items wherever you are. And the best part? These items are saved for offline access, so if you don't have access to a network you can still catch up on your saves. A hidden feature in the apps is that they give you five quick pieces that you can read, which can help when you are short or time but want to review items on your list.

To make things even easier, Pocket is integrated with over 500 other applications. That means that when you are reading tweets, catching up on blog posts, or browsing the Web, Pocket is integrated into other programs, allowing you to more easily save items.

POCKET IN THE CLASSROOM

In order to use Pocket, users must have an email address and be over the age of 13, unless parent permission is obtained. The requirement to have an email address will prevent some educators from using the service. However, a teacher could create a classroom account where he or she saves sites for the class. Since you can make what you share public, this could be a great option if you cannot give students their own accounts. Another use might be for a school leader and staff to have access to a shared account where they can all save resources.

REFLECTION ACTIVITY

1. Sign up for a free Pocket account. Practice using it with the blogs you are reading each week by adding posts that you want to read later.
2. Review the items you've saved in your Pocket account. Move between your Unread and Read lists to get a feel for how it works.
3. Think back to the Chapter 5 Reflection activity. Download the Diigo Browser extension. Once you've added an item to Pocket, use the Diigo Extension to save items from Pocket to Diigo.

Other Tools for Curation

As we've seen, there are three main tools that I use to accomplish all tasks related to curation and sharing. But, as we know, using just three tools can be tricky for a few reasons.

For starters, Web 2.0 tools come and go. Take Diigo. Diigo wasn't always the most popular social bookmarking service. Delicious was the major player in the early days of social bookmarking. When I started using a social bookmarking service, I was using Delicious because everyone else was using it too. Then Delicious was bought by Yahoo and was changed so much I had to find something else. Eventually Delicious was sold again, only to be shut down briefly and then returned under a similar name with similar features. But by then, most users, including me, had moved to Diigo.

Second, Web tools add features all the time. Evernote is nothing close to the service it was when it started. It has only gotten better over time. The same is true with several of the tools in this chapter. While they started out as something simple, all have added features that have made them better.

The point is, web tools come and go and change often, so it's always good to have at least an understanding of the tools that are out there.

> By knowing what is available to you, it's easy to swap out the tools in your toolbox or find the right tool for the right job.

Here are several other tools that can be used for curation. They are great for either finding resources or sharing what you've found. Some are great for both. But all are worth checking out.

PINTEREST

http://pinterest.com

I will admit that, for the longest time, I didn't really understand Pinterest. I was eating a lot of great things that my family was finding there, but I didn't see the value in the education space. Gradually, I came around and realized that, for some, it can be a place to find some wonderful classroom design resources, lesson ideas, and more. Many educators are using it as a starting place when looking for help with teaching difficult concepts or when they need an idea for completing a project. The visual nature of Pinterest appeals to a lot of people.

Using Pinterest is easy. Browse to what you want to "pin" and, either by using the browser extension or by manually creating the "pin," you save the resource along with an image to a "board." Many pinners have several boards for a variety of subjects. Think of boards as being similar to the tags that we used in Diigo. Boards are a way to organize your pins so you can find what you've saved.

Check out the website "25 of the Best Pinterest Boards to Follow for Educators" to see how various educators are using Pinterest to curate resources and information:

http://www.teachthought.com/social-media/25-of-the-best-pinterest-boards-in-education/

EDUCLIPPER

http://educlipper.net

Created by the talented Adam Bellow, this site is similar to Pinterest in that you "clip" resources and add them to a board; however, this site is dedicated to educational resources. Since Pinterest is geared toward the general public, there is a lot of junk there. This is not the case with EduClipper. The resources curated here are for the classroom and for students, so you will find a treasure trove of resources for learning and growing.

There are lots of features for educators like creating classes and importing students, which will allow your students to use it as well. EduClipper is one tool that you'll definitely want to check out.

STORIFY

http://storify.com

As we've seen, Twitter can be a great place to find resources, but sharing resources from a hashtag can be a challenge. Storify does all the work for you by finding specific tweets or hashtags from Twitter and presenting them in a visually appealing format. But it doesn't stop at tweets. You can pull in videos from YouTube, photos from Instagram, Google search results, and even other webpages. If you are looking for an easy way to share curated resources from a variety of sources, check out Storify.

Want to see what others are creating? Check out the featured stories and users or search for specific topics or stories to find exactly what you are looking for.

IFTTT

http://ifttt.com

There is simply no end to the flow of information available on the Internet. When it comes to trying to organize it and do something with it, you may run into some challenges. I know that I regularly am looking for ways to make that process better.

IFTTT (an acronym for "If This, Then That") is a lot like coding. If something happens in one place, then something happens in another place. The "something" could be an action on the Internet, an action that you take in your email, or something else. I think that where IFTTT really shines is in its ability to curate information and organize the curation process. Setting up "recipes" to automatically send information to specific places, locate new information, or more quickly organize that information can lead to better curation.

There are some recipes that you'll want to check out to make your curation of resources easier and more organized:

- **Twitter Favorites to Evernote.** If you are like me, you are getting loads of great content and resources from Twitter. The simple way to make save the stuff you find there is to favorite those tweets. But the big flaw is that, if the tweet gets deleted, so does your favorite. Another flaw is that you can't search. You'll want to get those favorites out of Twitter and into somewhere more user-friendly. When you favorite something on Twitter, the tweet and all its contents get sent to a notebook that you specify in Evernote. Once it's in Evernote, you can search it, tag it, and do so much more with it. Not an

Evernote user? Not to worry. You can send those favorites to a Google Spreadsheet.

- **RSS to Email.** I was a big fan of Google Reader before it shut down. Since then, I've moved away from using an RSS reader and find most of my information on Twitter. But that doesn't mean that RSS isn't still useful. Using the RSS feed for any webpage, you can have new content sent to your email as it happens. While you probably wouldn't want to use it on content that changes constantly, you could set up a search for a particular type of content or news event and, when new items are added, you'll get an email. This is great for students doing real-time research on events happening now. Email not your thing? You can save those RSS items to Pocket too.

- **Sending the Daily Weather to Other Programs.** As a science teacher, I am all about data. Having practical, real-life data for my students was always better than made-up data from the textbook. Weather was always a great source for data. There are loads of weather recipes, allowing you to send the weather data to spreadsheets in order to analyze trends over time or simply to be notified when there is rain. These can be really helpful for capturing easy data.

- **Sending Fitbit Data to Other Programs.** Using Fitbit is an easy way to keep track of fitness goals. Many of my friends who are physical education teachers are using Fitbit to help their kids stay aware of how active they are and how they can improve their fitness. IFTTT has several recipes that allow you to export data from Fitbit into a spreadsheet, Evernote, or somewhere else so you can analyze or manipulate the information.

A new feature is "Collections." These are sets of premade recipes that instantly give you lots of options. One of the best collections is "Recipes for Following the News," which includes all the necessary recipes for doing just that. Again, great for keeping up with real-time events.

THINGLINK

http://thinglink.com/edu

If we think back to our example of the museum curator, the last part of his or her job is to put the gathered resources into some sort of order to tell a story. Curators want to draw people in and help them to become part of that story. When we want to do the same with our curated resources, I can think of nothing more visual than ThingLink.

ThingLink starts with an image. Images can conjure up all sorts of emotions, so finding an image that adds to the story of the resources that you want to share is key. The next step is to click on various parts of the image to add in your resources. You can include links to additional images, videos, or websites that help you to tell the story of the image or share your resources in a dynamic way.

Think about an image of Amelia Earhart standing in front of her plane before setting off on her tragic journey. The image of Earhart herself could be tagged with links to her biography and her story, while the image of the plane could be tagged with a map of the journey along with the theories surrounding the plane's disappearance. The picture sets the stage for the story, and the links that the image contains help to tell the story.

ThingLink offers free accounts for educators that has all the features of a regular account but also adds the ability to easily create student accounts.

FLIPBOARD

http://flipboard.com

Built for your Apple, Windows, or Android device, Flipboard is a handy app that takes some of the guesswork out of curation on your mobile device. Using a slick magazine layout, you tell Flipboard what types of topics you are looking for or enter a specific source of information, and Flipboard will feed you with a constant supply of quality content.

In the search field, you will find the ability to look for things like topics, specific magazines, curators who are sharing their information, or other publishers. The resources are vast, and you can find virtually anything on any topic you are looking for.

One of my favorite publishers and curators is the team over at AnEsturary.com. This team is constantly curating great articles related to all things education and sharing them through the profile *FieldFlips* (http://flip.it/nZoxr)

One of the best features is that you can integrate your social media accounts not only to share the great content you find but also to allow Flipboard to curate your Twitter, Facebook, and other social media feeds. Flipboard will go through and find the stuff people are sharing the most and add it to a board that you can flip through at your leisure. No need to worry about missing the great blog posts everyone is reading or the website everyone is sharing. Flipboard will find it for your and make sure you don't miss it.

REFLECTION ACTIVITY

Review all the tools, apps, and sites from this section. Based on what you've read, pick one that you want to use. Commit to signing up and using it. In your Evernote notebook, reflect on your experience. What worked well? What didn't? Will you continue to use the tool? Do this for four to six weeks.

Curation in the Classroom

As we've learned, curation is an important part of our learning as professionals. Curation also needs to be an important skill that we teach to our students as well. My middle school students were wonderful to teach. Their organization skills, however, were quite lacking. And really I can't blame them. Before they came to me, they never really had to do much organizing. Their teachers did that for them.

Take one of the most common digital lessons we see in an elementary classroom, the "web quest." The idea is that the teacher has some sort of learning content that they want students to explore through a series of websites. The teacher provides the students with all of the necessary websites and lists the steps that the students will need to take in order to locate the information. The students then follow the steps and repeat the information that they find.

Very little to no curation takes place on the part of the students. The teacher does all the work for them by choosing the websites and listing the exact steps that the students need to take to find the information. This sort of activity is more of an exercise in testing whether students can follow exact directions rather than being an effective way of teaching them how to curate learning content.

Now, I'm not saying that all web quests are like this. Some are better designed than others. My point here is that in elementary and even sometimes in middle school and high school, we see very little emphasis on helping students to develop the good curation skills that they are going to need later in life. Think back to what Howard Rheingold said. The need to have a well-developed filter to examine the information that we see every day is quickly becoming more important than some of the skills on which we spend so much time and effort in schools.

The development of curation skills can start as early as kindergarten and can build and grow as the students move through the grades so that, as they get older and the research gets more challenging and the need for good curation skills becomes greater, they will be able to handle vast amounts of information with ease.

Let's take a look at the three steps in the curation process and how they can be fostered in the classroom.

FINDING AND STORING THE RIGHT INFORMATION

As students embark on their quest to find information for a project or lesson, many do just as we all do. They go to Google or another search engine, type in the topic that their teacher has given them, and click on the first link. They read the first paragraph and, many times without giving it much thought, begin to copy down what they see. Even worse, they don't have a good system to save that information so they can go back to it.

The fact is, we as educators don't spend a great deal of time teaching students the essential information literacy skills that are needed to filter their searches in order to find more specific information. We get so focused on ensuring that they are learning the content that we miss critical opportunities to teach them valuable and important skills that they can use no matter what they are learning.

The same tricks that we saw in Chapter 2 to limit our searches can be taught to students. One of the easiest tricks is to use the advanced search options. Students should be familiar with how advanced search works and how it can help them find the best information quickly.

Google has a great series of lesson plans for students at all grade levels that cover topics like choosing the right search terms, using search operators, and understanding search results (http://www .google.com/insidesearch/searcheducation/lessons.html). These lessons are a great way to introduce students to these concepts, but the conversations have to be ongoing and embedded throughout the curriculum.

Not only do students need to be able to find information, they have to be able to store it and organize it so they can go back to it later. All of the tools that we covered in the previous chapters can work in the classroom. As we saw, there are many specific tools for educators that can be used to create accounts for students and more. Investigate these tools, not just on your own but with your students as well.

One method that I have seen used with great success is to divide the class up into smaller groups so that, over the course of a few weeks, the students get to try each of the three tools. Each time the students work with a tool, they have a similar set of questions to answer in order to put the tool through its paces. After everyone has had an opportunity to try all three tools, they report back on successes and challenges. Not only are students getting an opportunity to learn how to use the best tool for them, they are learning how to evaluate technology and see its role in the learning process.

ACCURACY IN INFORMATION

I can remember one project in particular that illustrates the importance of accurate information. Had I spent more time talking to students about how to find the most accurate information, the project would have turned out much better for all of us.

As a science teacher, one of the topics that I most enjoyed teaching was chemistry. Mr. Wizard was my hero, so I enjoyed showing chemical reactions and talking about atoms. By far, my most favorite topic in chemistry was the periodic table. It was fascinating to me. I wanted my students to see what I saw, so each student got to pick an element that they had to investigate. Their job was to research the element fully and then present that information to the class.

We went to the media center, and I set them loose. Some went straight for the computers and ultimately ended up copying their information from Wikipedia. Others went to the encyclopedias that hadn't been updated in many, many years. The students worked feverishly to get all of the necessary information.

When the time came to present their information, we discovered that the accuracy of information varied widely among the students. Several students had picked the same elements, and none of their information matched. One student would have one number for an atomic weight, while another student would have a completely different number. The same was true for many of the facts that they had to present.

This turned into a great teachable moment for me as it illustrated that the students didn't really have the skills that good scientists should have when it comes to looking at information. Students and scientists need to be able to find information and then verify it for accuracy.

As educators, we've all seen the same thing. We assign students something to research and, before we can finish our thought, they have already clicked on the first link on Google and are ready to regurgitate the information back to us. Very little thought goes into that click or how good the information is.

This part of information literacy used to be a skill that was covered only when students went to the library to find information. Now that they have access to that information at their fingertips through a device in their hands, these conversations around the accuracy of information (and the other parts of digital literacy) have to be ongoing and embedded into our curriculum.

How can you get the evaluation of information conversation started? There are a couple of simple lesson plans you can use and/or adapt:

- **Kathy Schrock's Critical Evaluation of a Web Page** (http://www.schrockguide.net/critical-evaluation-lesson-plan.html). In this lesson, students brainstorm what makes a great website and then compare their own list to a set list of what all websites should have. Students then learn how to examine a webpage and are given several examples of "fake" websites to determine just how good the information is.

- **Google's Evaluating Credibility of Sources** (http://bit.ly/googlesourceeval). In this lesson, students work to determine what makes information on the web credible and how can they easily determine whether or not a website is credible. They also discuss how opinion can influence credibility and how to separate fact from opinion when it comes to web resources.

These are one-shot lesson plans. The conversations around the accuracy and credibility of information found on the Internet needs to be ongoing. Once students have the skills, you should simply reinforce the skill by presenting them with information and asking them how they know that it is accurate and credible. The more students have the opportunity to practice, the better they will get at evaluating information on their own.

SHARING OUR LEARNING

Think back to when you were in school. Inevitably, you had a large paper or essay to write. You'd spend hours crafting the right words and organizing your thoughts. The day would come for you to turn in your work, only to receive it back a few days later with a grade on it, perhaps with little feedback. And then it was over. The paper ended up in the bottom of your bag; in a folder somewhere, never to be seen again; or in the trash, lost forever. What if your words could have changed history or had been a breakthrough that could have improved the world?

OK. Chances are, your words might not have done either of those things. But wouldn't it have been nice for more than just the teacher and your classmates to have seen your work and potentially benefitted from it? That learning doesn't have to stay just between the student and the teacher.

The same should be true with the information and resources that students are curating. Just as educators can benefit from what their colleagues curate, students can benefit from what their fellow students curate. The information can be reviewed, remixed, and reused in new ways to create new knowledge.

Think back to all the of the tools that we discussed earlier. Each had a sharing component that made it easy to let the world know what we were saving and why we saved it. And many of the student-friendly tools have built-in features that make this process easier. Take the student accounts in Diigo. When a teacher creates student accounts, whatever resources those students save get added to the class group. Sharing is built in because it is important. Emphasize the need for students to share their learning and encourage them to use these features to do so.

1. How are you currently encouraging students to curate information in your class? Are the methods that you are using effective?

2. How do the curation methods that you are using compare with what has been described here?

3. What role does information literacy play in your classroom? Do students understand how to validate their information?

CHAPTER
9

Wrapping It All Up

A s I hope you've discovered, content curation is more than just gathering resources to use in a lesson plan or a video to use as a teaching aid. Curation is a part of the information literacy process with which all of us (students and educators) need to be familiar. Simply discovering information isn't enough. We need to have a purpose to our search. We need to understand how to be better searchers of information. We need to check our information for accuracy and credibility. We need to have a good tool with which to store that information, and we need to share that information with the world.

As Howard Rheingold says:

> To me, the issue of information literacy could be even more important than the health or education of some individuals. Fundamental aspects of democracy, economic production, and the discovery and use of knowledge might be at stake. Some of the biggest problems facing the world today seem to be far beyond the ability

of any individual or community, or even the whole human race, to tackle. . . . Although large forces are at work, when it comes to the shape of online media, I believe that what people know—and how many people know—matters. Digital media and networked publics are only the infrastructure for participation—the cables and chips do no good unless people know how to use them. (http://blog.sfgate.com/rheingold/2009/06/30/crap-detection-101/)

Curation is an essential skill for not only students and educators so that they can be better learners, it is also an essential skill for us all so that we can be better, more informed consumers of information and so that we can use that knowledge and understanding to work on the most challenging issues facing us today. Something simple like finding the best information, storing it, and sharing it can be powerful.

What will you curate today?

More importantly, how will you share what you curate with the world?

Resources

Chapter 2

Information Literacy

- Understanding Information Literacy: A Primer http://www
.unesco.org/new/en/communication-and-information/
resources/publications-and-communication-materials/publi
cations/full-list/understanding-information-literacy-a-primer/
- American Library Association: Introduction to Information
Literacy http://www.ala.org/acrl/issues/infolit/overview/intro
- Project Information Literacy: http://projectinfolit.org/

Chapter 3

Some Blogs to Get You Started

- Blogging About the Web 2.0 Connected Classroom—Steven
W. Anderson: http://blog.web20classroom.org
- My Island View—Tom Whitby: http://tomwhitby.wordpress
.com
- Learning Is Leading—Kyle Pace: http://kylepace.com
- Cool Cat Teacher Blog—Vicki Davis: http://coolcatteacher
.blogspot.com/
- Kleinspiration—Erin Klein: http://www.kleinspiration.com/

Learning About Twitter Hashtags and Chats

- Cybraryman's List of Twitter Hashtags: http://www.cybrary
man.com/edhashtags.html

- Why Twitter Chats Matter: http://blog.web20classroom
  .org/2014/05/why-twitter-chats-matter.html
- A Brief History of #Edchat: http://blog.web20classroom.org
  /2012/03/brief-history-of-edchat.html
- Some More Twitter Chats Worth Checking Out: http://blog
  .web20classroom.org/2012/04/some-more-twitter-chats-
  worth-checking.html

Chapter 4

Evernote Resources

- Evernote101:http://www.youtube.com/watch?v=XjJviCF69GQ
- Evernote for Educators: http://www.livebinders.com/play/
  play/245623
- 10 Evernote Tips for School: http://blog.evernote.com/
  blog/2010/12/15/10-evernote-tips-for-school-education-series/
- Evernote for Schools: https://evernote.com/schools/

Chapter 5

Diigo Resources

- Diigo 101: https://www.youtube.com/watch?v=o0FTC_PAwnE
- Why Diigo Rocks: http://blog.web20classroom.org/2011/10/
  why-diigo-rocks.html
- Student Learning With Diigo: https://sites.google.com/site/
  team8project9440/using-diigo-in-the-classroom-2

Chapter 6

Pocket Resources

- Pocket 101: http://help.getpocket.com/customer/portal/arti
  cles/1668192-getting-started-with-pocket-on-your-computer
- Pocket App Directory: http://getpocket.com/apps/

A SAGE Company

Corwin is committed to improving education for all learners by publishing books and other professional development resources for those serving the field of PreK–12 education. By providing practical, hands-on materials, Corwin continues to carry out the promise of its motto: **"Helping Educators Do Their Work Better."**